I0896295

Judy Blume

THE NIX

Judy Blume

Tales of a Timeless Children's Author

Colleen Sexton

LERNER PUBLICATIONS ◆ MINNEAPOLIS

Lerner Publications Company
An imprint of Lerner Publishing Group, Inc.
241 First Avenue North
Minneapolis, MN 55401 USA

For reading levels and more information, look up this title at www.lernerbooks.com.

Main body text set in Rotis Serif Std 55 Regular. Typeface provided by Adobe Systems.

Designer: Lauren Cooper **Photo Editor:** Sarah Whitt

Library of Congress Cataloging-in-Publication Data

Names: Sexton, Colleen A., 1967– author
Title: Judy Blume : tales of a timeless children's author / Colleen Sexton.
Description: Minneapolis : Lerner Publications, 2026. | Series: Gateway biographies | Includes bibliographical references and index. | Audience: Ages 9–14 | Audience: Grades 4–6 | Summary: "Readers explore the life of Judy Blume, beloved author whose work captures the complexity of growing up. Discover the person behind books such as *Tales of a Fourth Grade Nothing*, *Superfudge*, and many more"— Provided by publisher.
Identifiers: LCCN 2025022942 (print) | LCCN 2025022943 (ebook) | ISBN 9798765669341 library binding | ISBN 9798765684092 paperback | ISBN 9798765677414 epub
Subjects: LCSH: Blume, Judy—Juvenile literature | Authors, American—20th century—Biography—Juvenile literature | Children's literature—Authorship—Juvenile literature | LCGFT: Biographies | Literature.
Classification: LCC PS3552.L843 Z84 2026 (print) | LCC PS3552.L843 (ebook) | DDC 813/.54 [B]—dc23/eng/20250514

LC record available at https://lccn.loc.gov/2025022942
LC ebook record available at https://lccn.loc.gov/2025022943

Manufactured in the United States of America
1-1012819-53905-8/27/2025

TABLE OF CONTENTS

Judy Blume attending the *Are You There God? It's Me, Margaret* film premiere on April 15, 2023

On a warm spring evening in 2023, crowds gathered outside the Tropic Cinema in Key West, Florida. The theater's pink neon sign glowed. Below it, a marquee announced a special film screening of *Are You There God? It's Me, Margaret.* The movie's stars chatted with the press and waved to the crowd. But the real star there that night was Judy Blume, who wrote the beloved novel of the same name.

This night's celebration was decades in the making for Blume and that breakthrough book published in 1970. The title character, eleven-year-old Margaret Simon, talks to God as she struggles to grow up with a changing body. She shares her problems and asks God to help solve them. Blume wasn't sure that the book would ever be made into a movie. "The idea that this day has come, that it's finally here and that I'm here to see it makes me very happy, very proud, very nostalgic," Blume told the media there to cover the event.

Rachel McAdams (*left*) and Abby Ryder Fortson (*right*), stars of the film *Are You There God? It's Me, Margaret*, pose with Judy Blume (*center*).

Nearby, a reporter interviewed the stars of the film, Rachel McAdams and Abby Ryder Fortson. "When I first read the book, I was like . . . this is it. This is the experience we all go through," Fortson said. "I was so excited when I got the opportunity to bring Margaret to life because it's just something that we can all feel connected to, no matter who you are in this world."

Over the years, millions of young people around the world have read Blume's literary classic and felt that same connection. They know the author understands what it feels like to be a kid. Through empathy and humor, her honest writing has inspired and comforted readers.

Many of those readers, now adults, eagerly awaited the film version of the book that meant so much to them. As excited ticket holders poured into the theater and took their seats, Blume beamed. She hoped the audience would be happy with the film.

Early Years

Judith Sussman was born on February 12, 1938, in Elizabeth, New Jersey, where her parents grew up. Her father, Rudolph, worked as a dentist. Her mother, Esther, stayed home to care for Judy and her older brother, David. The family lived in a two-story brick house in a quiet neighborhood.

World War II (1939–1945) marked Judy's early childhood. In the evenings, the radio blared news of battles overseas. She heard about Nazi violence against Jews in Germany and other European countries. When she went to the movies, she saw Nazi leader Adolf Hitler in newsreels that played before the start of films back then. It was a scary time, especially because she was Jewish. Her mother tried to reassure her, telling her nothing like that could happen to them. But now she knew that this was something that could happen in the world.

Judy was shy and fearful. Her fears included dogs, swimming, and thunderstorms. Whenever she was scared, she looked to her father for comfort. She remembers games of hide-and-seek and their bedtime routine of hugs and kisses. Her father was funny, creative, and loving. Judy adored him. “He tried to raise me to want an adventurous life and to be adventurous and to take chances,” Judy recalled.

Judy’s quiet, serious mother was cautious and kept her feelings to herself. But she loved reading and filled the family’s home with books. She took young Judy to the library every week. Judy loved everything about books, from the way they looked to the way they smelled. “[My mother] let me sit on the floor and pull books out and look at them and sniff them,” Judy recalled. Her favorite books included *Madeline*, the Nancy Drew mysteries, and the Betsy-Tacy series. But no books were off-limits. As she grew, she read any book that interested her.

Judy had a big imagination. She made up dramatic stories with her dolls as the main characters. She spent hours bouncing a rubber ball against the side of the house, ideas turning in her mind. Some stories came from her feeling that adults kept secrets from kids. Judy hated that. Her imagination came to life thinking about what those secrets could be.

Judy dreamed of being an actor, a cowgirl, or a spy. Despite all the time she spent making up stories, she never thought about being a writer. “I didn’t know anything about writers,” Judy remembered. “It never occurred to me they were regular people and that I could grow up to become one, even though I loved to make up stories inside my head.”

When she was nine years old, Judy moved with her

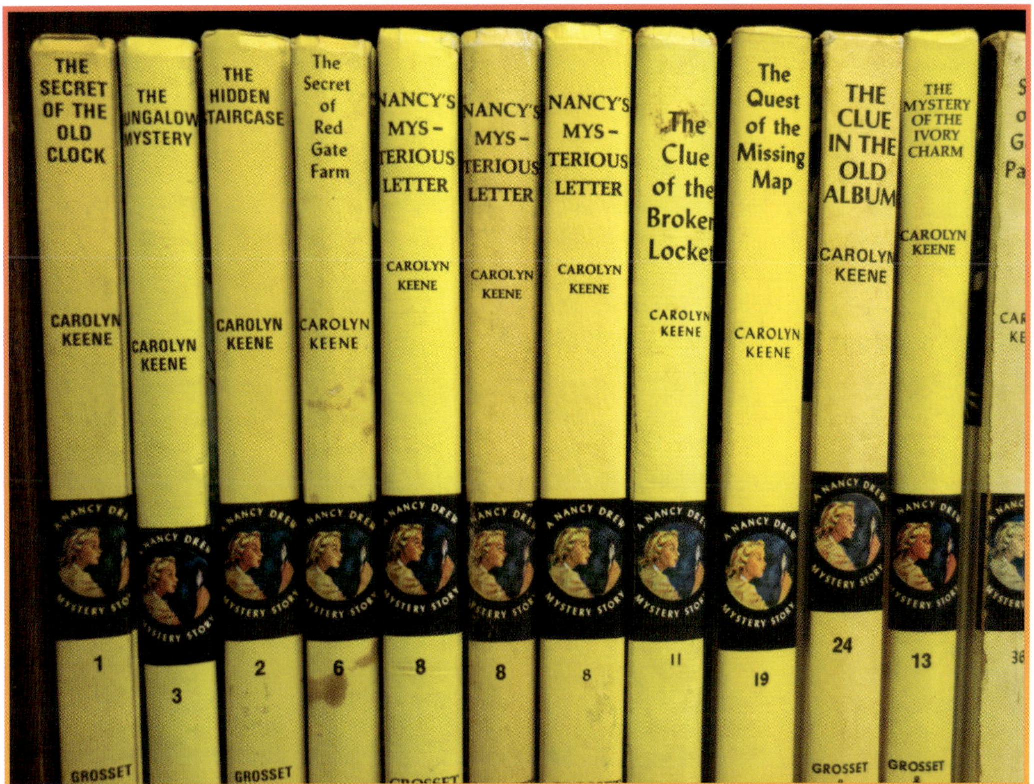

Nancy Drew mystery books were among Judy's favorites growing up.

mother, brother, and grandmother to Miami Beach, Florida, for a little while. Her brother was ill, and they hoped the warmer climate would improve his health. Her father stayed behind but flew down for visits. It was hard to be separated from him. At first, Judy struggled. She worried about her father being alone back home. And after two of her uncles died, Judy's worry became overwhelming. She prayed, making bargains with God to keep her father safe and healthy.

Miami Beach in 1949

But she also had fun in Florida. She made new friends, took ballet lessons, went roller skating, and swam in the ocean. She remembered playing outside all day. "We were free-range kids so we could play outside until our parents called us in," Judy recalled. "That helped me, I think, changed me to become more self-reliant and much less fearful."

When she returned to New Jersey, Judy was more outgoing. She sang in the school chorus, danced, and acted in plays. She also found a tight-knit group of friends. Heading into their teenage years, the girls talked about everything, from school and boys to how their bodies were changing.

Judy felt pressure from 1950s society to be pretty, talented, and popular. She also felt pressure from her mother to be perfect. But as hard as she tried, she knew she wasn't. Sometimes, all she could do was pretend for her mother, even when she didn't want to. She kept a lot of her feelings deep inside.

As she graduated from the all-girls Battin High School, Judy knew what was expected of her next. Her family wanted her to get a degree in case she ever needed to find a job, but they also wanted her to find someone she could marry. With these possibilities in mind, Judy headed off to college.

Wife and Mother

Judy Sussman attended New York University in Manhattan. During her sophomore year in 1958, she met law student John Blume. A New Jersey native like her, he was six years older and planned to work at his father's law firm.

The couple soon became engaged. Sussman was excited for her future. "I didn't know who I was or what I wanted, and he was already a lawyer," she recalled. "I was marrying a grown-up. And I was going to be a grown-up too."

New York University dormitory Judson Hall as seen from Washington Square Park in 1961

Five weeks before her wedding in August 1959, Sussman's worst childhood fear came true. Her father had a heart attack and died. Still stunned from his loss, she married John in a backyard ceremony. She knew her father would want her to move forward. The new

Mrs. Blume was twenty-one years old and beginning a marriage. But it was hard to be happy without her father.

In 1961 Blume earned a degree in early childhood education. But she didn't start a career. She focused on being a wife and then a mother. That year the Blumes welcomed a daughter, Randy, followed two years later by a son, Larry. By then, the family had moved into a four-bedroom home in the wealthy suburb of Scotch Plains, New Jersey.

Keeping the house tidy and caring for her children filled Blume's days. But as her children grew, she had more spare time and became bored. She didn't like shopping or playing tennis at the local country club like other women in the neighborhood. She didn't have much in common with them at all. But it was the 1960s and the women's movement was growing. Blume noticed that many women were starting to pursue their passions and activities that made them happy. She wanted to do something too.

While reading bedtime stories to Randy and Larry, Blume wondered if she could write children's books. Ideas tumbled in her head. One day, she started putting her thoughts to paper. She doodled and played around with rhymes. Blume remembered the childhood joy of creating stories.

One day a brochure from New York University arrived in the mail. It listed a night class called Writing for Children and Teenagers. Blume signed up. She felt as if the course was meant just for her.

The Women's Movement

In the mid-1900s, women didn't have many opportunities to be leaders or to follow their dreams. Women had struggled for equal rights for years, but the cause gained strength after author and activist Betty Friedan wrote a book called *The Feminine Mystique* in 1963. It showed women who felt unhappy in their traditional roles as wives and mothers that they weren't alone.

Women started speaking out and standing up for their rights. They demanded that they be treated equally to men at work and in schools. They worked to get unfair laws changed. "Those of us who call ourselves feminists and came of age in the women's movement . . . wanted to be free in the way that men were free," Blume remembered. While the efforts of these feminists opened new doors for many women, the fight for fairness continues.

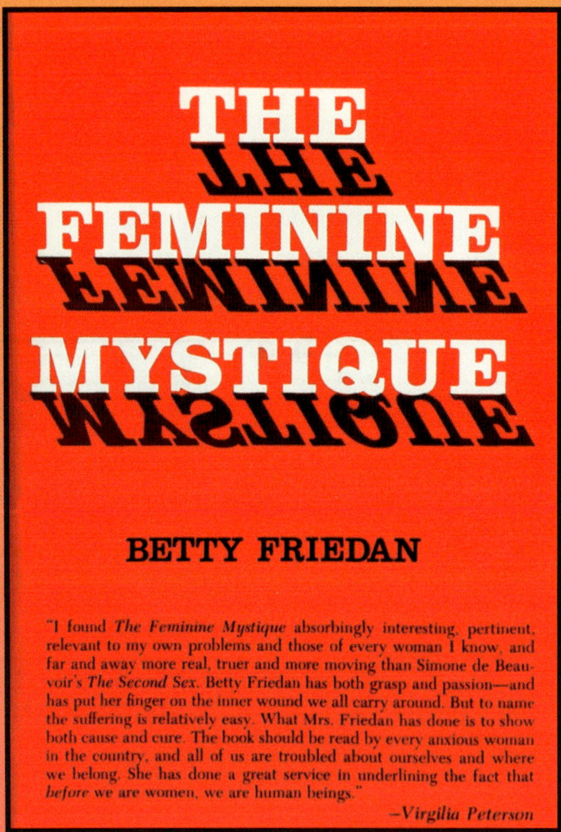

Becoming an Author

Every Monday evening, Blume hopped on a bus to New York City so she could attend her writing class. It became the most exciting part of her life. The small class was led by children's book author Lee Wyndham. Wyndham listed many rules for writing children's books. But Blume quickly broke them and pursued her own ideas.

Each week Blume looked forward to receiving feedback on her work. Wyndham gave her a lot of encouragement. Blume felt lucky to have such a supportive teacher, even if they didn't always agree. She didn't mind the criticism Wyndham occasionally provided. It was always given in a positive way.

But Blume didn't get the same positive response from her family and friends. They thought her writing was just a hobby. Her husband joked that writing was better than spending money on shopping. Blume felt resentment from neighbors who wondered why she couldn't just try to fit in and be like them. And some people discouraged her from writing. They told her it was unlikely she would succeed. But she didn't let that stop her.

When her class ended, Blume signed up again, eager to keep getting feedback on her work. She was determined to become a published author. Blume sent many stories to every major publisher, receiving rejection after rejection. Even though she cried after her first rejection, Blume was able to bounce back. After her second rejection, she was eager to show them what else she had to share, whether they liked it or not.

Blume wrote every day while her children were at school. In class, Wyndham commented on her strength in writing realistic fiction. That gave Blume the courage to start a novel called *Iggie's House*, which was inspired by the civil rights movement of the 1960s. Blume wrote about a Black family that moves into a white suburban neighborhood. She brought a new chapter to class each week.

One day in 1969, Blume's dream finally came true. She received a call from a company that wanted to publish one of her stories. It was called *The One in the Middle Is the Green Kangaroo*. This picture book tells the story of a family's middle child, Freddy Dissel, who is tired of feeling left out. Blume was so excited that she whooped in celebration. She would be a published author at last. And it was just the beginning. She was ready for her new career.

Writing *Margaret*

In the 1960s, most books for children featured simple stories with happy endings. They often taught a lesson. But Dick Jackson and Bob Verrone of Bradbury Press had a different idea. They were looking for stories set in the real world with characters that sounded like real people. In Blume, the publishers found an author with the same goal. They decided to publish *Iggie's House* and began a longtime relationship with Blume.

With Jackson as her editor, Blume was eager to start her next book. She thought about what it was like to be a girl in sixth grade. "I remember being that age. I was fascinated by the idea of changing bodies," Blume said. "I wanted to write the truth, the reality of being that age." It took only six weeks at her typewriter to draft *Are You There God? It's Me, Margaret.* There was something different about this book for Blume. As she drafted, she realized this was a whole new experience. "For the first time since I'd started writing, I let go and this story came pouring out," Blume said. "I felt as if I'd always known Margaret."

Are You There God? It's Me, Margaret **is special to many Blume fans.**

In the book, Margaret Simon moves from New York to New Jersey. As she starts attending a new school and making new friends, she worries about fitting in. She has a lot of questions about how her body is changing during puberty. Is she normal? At the same time, she's struggling with religion. Her mother was raised Christian, and her father was raised Jewish. Where does she belong? Margaret begins talking to God, sharing her worries about school, her friends, boys, bras, and getting her period. She asks for God's help.

Blume wrote honestly and realistically about Margaret's emotions and experiences. She shared how it feels to be between childhood and adulthood. "You're on the cusp, when things are going to change and things are going to happen," Blume said. "And you still don't know everything and you're curious." Thoughts and feelings like Margaret's had not been explored in a children's book. Young readers were excited to see their own struggles reflected on the page.

Are You There God? It's Me, Margaret arrived in bookstores in 1970. Some reviewers took issue with the topics Blume wrote about. They didn't think it was appropriate for kids to read about Margaret's obsession with her changing body and her struggle with religion. But many more reviewers found the book refreshing. The *New York Times* named it an Outstanding Book of the Year.

Young readers agreed. Margaret's story rang true to their lives, and they felt as if Blume understood them.

Blume speaks with young readers in 1977.

Young fans crowded bookstores for Blume's book signings. "Margaret brought me my first and most loyal readers," Blume said. "I love her for that."

Finding Success

Blume had found her voice. Margaret let Blume see who she was and who she wanted to be. Ideas for new books buzzed in Blume's head. She jotted them down whenever they came to her–in notebooks, on shopping lists, and on tissues. And she wrote constantly. Over the next five years, Blume authored eight books.

Blume continued to tell stories about unexplored issues that connected with young readers. In *Then Again Maybe I Won't*, twelve-year-old Tony struggles with his changing body as well as changes in his family when newfound wealth prompts them to move to an upscale neighborhood. *It's Not the End of the World* deals with the issue of divorce, which was on the rise in the 1970s. It describes how twelve-year-old Karen copes as her parents' marriage ends. *Deenie* tells the story of a beautiful teenager whose mother pressures her to be a model. But Deenie develops scoliosis, a disorder that causes her spine to curve and requires her to wear a back brace to correct it.

Every day in the quiet hours after her children left for school, Blume tapped out stories on her typewriter. She loved that time. She was able to write book after book. Randy became her first reader. After school, she scooped up the pages her mother had just written. Blume was eager to know what her daughter thought and what made her laugh.

Randy also gave Blume ideas. After she described a bullying incident at school, Blume wrote *Blubber.* In this book, fifth-grader Jill goes along with her classmates when they bully an overweight classmate. Then she finds herself a target of bullying. At that time, people usually didn't talk about bullying in schools. Blume wrote *Forever* after another talk with Randy. Her daughter wished for a book about teenagers in love that didn't end badly, as many teen books did at that time. Blume penned the story of Katherine, a high school senior who experiences her first serious romantic relationship.

Blume also wrote more books for younger readers in the early 1970s. In *Freckle Juice*, Andrew makes a juice recipe that he hopes will give him freckles. Blume also started the Fudge series with *Tales of a Fourth Grade Nothing.* This book tackles the sibling rivalry between Peter Hatcher and his younger brother, Fudge. Next came the story of Peter's classmate Sheila in *Otherwise Known as Sheila the Great.* At summer camp, Sheila must face her many fears.

Fudge!

Judy Blume loves to make kids laugh. The antics of Peter Hatcher's little brother, Fudge, has done just that for generations of kids. The five funny books in the Fudge series include *Tales of a Fourth Grade Nothing, Otherwise Known as Sheila the Great, Superfudge, Fudge-a-mania*, and *Double Fudge*.

Blume based Fudge on her son, Larry, as a toddler. There is seemingly no end to the ways Fudge annoys and embarrasses Peter. Fudge swallows Peter's pet turtle. He disappears at a movie theater. He leaves his new shoes on the subway. He gets stuck in an elevator. And a frustrated Peter thinks he gets away with everything. Some of Blume's most popular and best-selling books, the Fudge series made her a star children's author.

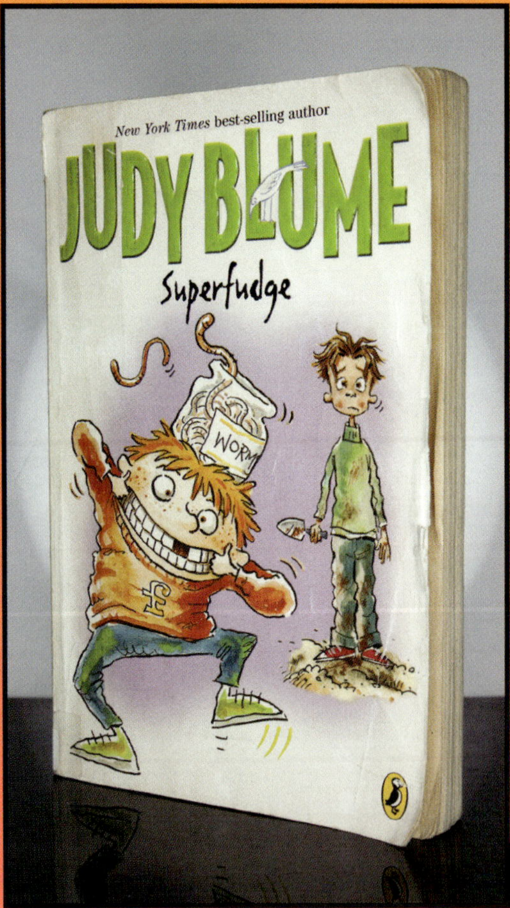

Superfudge by Judy Blume

By 1975 Blume had found great success as a writer. It brought her new challenges and fulfillment. But she was unhappy living the life of a suburban wife. After sixteen years of marriage, she asked John for a divorce. She and the children moved to Princeton, New Jersey. The divorce was hard on Randy and Larry. In time the family found a way to move forward with their new lives.

Blume's popularity continued to grow throughout the 1970s.

New Mexico

Blume was quickly becoming America's most famous children's author. Her popularity skyrocketed when Dell Publishing Company made a deal with Bradbury Press, the company that originally published Blume's books. Dell released Blume's books in paperback. A lower price and placement in racks at local drugstores made the titles more widely available to kids. They read the paperbacks over and over again and then passed the books on to their friends. By the end of 1976, Dell had printed more than 1.75 million copies of Blume's books.

That year was a whirlwind for Blume. She married Tom Kitchens, a scientist she had met on an airplane. Blume liked that he was curious and had a sense of adventure. For Kitchens's job, she and the children spent several months living in London, England. When Kitchens received a new assignment, they packed up their New Jersey home and moved to Los Alamos, New Mexico.

Los Alamos, New Mexico, where Blume lived for a time

Blume in 1979

It was a challenging time. Randy and Larry were unhappy about the marriage. They didn't like living in New Mexico. Blume had trouble making friends there and felt lonely. She wondered if it had been a mistake to marry Kitchens. They had known each other for only a short time.

Blume decided to focus on her writing. She put her own childhood experience into her next book, *Starring Sally J. Freedman as Herself*. Like young Judy, Sally and her family move to Miami in 1947 for her brother's health. Sally has a big imagination and makes up wild stories as she finds new friends and adventure in Florida.

Blume also surprised people by writing her first book for adults. Titled *Wifey*, it features Sandy, a wife and mother who is frustrated in those traditional roles. By the time the book was published in 1978, Blume had moved with her family to Santa Fe, New Mexico. *Wifey* became a bestseller. That same year, CBS aired a TV movie of Blume's novel *Forever*.

Blume's fame grew. But her success strained her marriage. Blume knew it wasn't working, and she and Kitchens divorced in 1978. Blume liked Santa Fe and decided to stay there while Randy and Larry finished high school. She later bought an apartment in Manhattan, the center of the publishing world, and shuttled back and forth between the two cities. Blume was forty years old, financially independent, and in control of her own life. But she wasn't prepared for what came next.

Censorship

In the 1970s, when Blume started writing, people felt free to explore new ideas and say what they thought. Blume always felt that she could write honestly. And kids responded, telling her in letters how much she helped them. With her books a mainstay on bestseller lists, Blume was firmly established as the country's favorite children's author. But things started to change in 1980.

That year Ronald Reagan was elected president of the United States. Many Americans supported the new

Ronald Reagan on the presidential campaign trail in November 1979

administration's desire for a society with more conservative, traditional values. Some parents started to worry about what their children were reading. They targeted Blume's books, saying that reading about changing bodies was offensive and harmful to children. They called her books immoral.

In many communities, parents started challenging Blume's books, demanding that schools and libraries remove them. At that time, libraries rarely had policies in place for dealing with book challenges. Confronted with angry parents, librarians often pulled Blume's books off the shelves.

Blume was stunned. She couldn't believe that there were people who thought reading certain books could be dangerous for young people. She realized certain groups thought they knew what was best for everyone, and they wanted to control what kids were reading. One group even published a pamphlet titled "How to Rid Your Schools and Libraries of Judy Blume Books."

Letters to Judy

At the height of her popularity, Judy Blume received about two thousand letters a week from kids. They told her their deepest thoughts, asked for advice, and shared what they loved about her books. She felt touched by how open kids were in their writings to her. It was clear that they felt they could share things with her that they couldn't share with their parents. Blume spent three years selecting letters and compiling them along with details from her own life into a book, *Letters to Judy: What Kids Wish They Could Tell You*. She dedicated it to all the young people who shared their lives with her.

When Dick Jackson read Blume's latest manuscript, *Tiger Eyes*, he was concerned. Set in New Mexico, it tells the story of how fifteen-year-old Davey tries to deal with her father's tragic death. The emotions echo Blume's own experience of losing her father. Davey also talks about her body and her feelings, parts that Jackson feared would get the book censored. "I got the message," Blume said. "If you leave in those lines, the censors will come after this book. Librarians and teachers won't buy it. . . . Everyone is too scared. The political climate has changed." She listened to her editor's advice, but it was hard to make changes she didn't believe in.

Blume kept writing through all the book bans. *Smart Women*, her second novel for adults, focuses on two divorced women and their daughters. She then shifted to writing for a younger audience. Inspired by Randy and Larry's childhood, *The Pain and the Great One* is about

Blume is best known as a children's author, but she also wrote about divorce and other tough topics for adult audiences.

sibling rivalry between eight-year-old Abigail (the Pain) and six-year-old Jake (the Great One). It kicked off a series that would include four more zany tales about the brother and sister. Her next book was *Just as Long as We're Together.* It features Stephanie, Rachel, and Allison, three best friends making their way through seventh grade. The same characters appear later in a follow-up novel titled *Here's to You, Rachel Robinson.*

Throughout the 1980s, Blume was the most banned author in the United States. She felt threatened and alone. But she defended herself to newspaper journalists and in TV interviews. Blume firmly believed that parents had the right to take books away from their own children, but they shouldn't be allowed to make that decision for all parents. Kids agreed. Many fought to keep Blume's books in their libraries. They spoke out at meetings, wrote letters, and collected signatures on petitions. And sometimes they won.

Banned Books Week

Every year Banned Books Week brings together members of the book community to draw national attention to the issue of censorship. Authors, publishers, teachers, librarians, and readers look for ways to fight book bans and share their cause with others.

The American Library Association (ALA) established the annual event in 1982, when censorship was on the rise. The ALA tracks book challenges around the country and highlights them during Banned Books Week. Challenges are once again rising. From 2001 to 2020, an average of about 270 titles per year faced challenges. In 2024 that number increased to more than 2,400 challenged titles in a single year.

Blume is a lifelong advocate for freedom of speech.

The Kids Fund

In 1981 Judy Blume established the Kids Fund. It gives grants to programs that help young people communicate openly with their parents. Many of Blume's projects helped raise money for the Kids Fund, particularly *The Judy Blume Diary*. Published in 1981, the rainbow-covered book featured quotes from Blume, photographs of kids, and lots of room for kids to write their thoughts.

Blume fought back too. She joined the advisory board of the National Coalition Against Censorship. Finally, she felt less alone. She had other people on her side. Blume was eager to fight for the authors and librarians who faced censorship. She wanted to do something that would have a positive impact. Fighting against censorship for all books made sense. She could help protect books.

A Literary Legacy

In 1987 family members gathered for a wedding on the terrace of Blume's apartment in New York City. Holding a bouquet of white flowers, Blume married George Cooper. "George is magic," Blume said. "He's a wonderful complement for me. . . . He's not a worrier. He's easygoing." He was a law professor. She had met him on a blind date in Santa Fe. His daughter, Amanda, along with Blume's children, who were now adults, formed a close family.

Blume with her husband, George Cooper, in 2016

Blume's life was happy and full of so much that she loved. She and her husband had moved to Connecticut. They enjoyed time at their summer place on Martha's Vineyard, an island off the coast of Massachusetts. Blume took up tap dancing. And she kept working. She and Larry, who had entered the movie business, created a film version of *Otherwise Known as Sheila the Great*. And by the early 1990s, Blume was a grandmother. She was thrilled when Randy, who became a therapist, gave birth to a boy named Elliot.

A few years later, Blume was looking for somewhere warm to work. She was writing *Summer Sisters*, a book for adults about the friendship between two young women over twenty summers. Blume and Cooper rented a house in Key West, Florida. They liked the sunny island so much that they moved there.

Blume and Cooper quickly felt at home in the tight-knit community known for attracting musicians, artists, and writers. Cooper started the nonprofit Tropic Cinema theater. Residents can still see independent films and movie classics there today. Blume enjoyed morning walks and pedaling her pink bike down palm-shaded streets. She wrote in an office overlooking a lush, tropical garden.

Blume poses with her final book, *In the Unlikely Event*, in June 2015.

In 2015, at age seventy-seven, Blume finished her last book, *In the Unlikely Event*. This adult novel is set against real-life events from her teenage years. Over three months in 1951 and

1952, three passenger airplanes crashed in her hometown. Blume explores how these disasters affect three families. When she finished the book, she decided to stop writing. "I never ever miss it. Isn't that funny?" Blume said. "It was my life for so long, and it changed my life, and it gave me my life."

The next year, Blume and Cooper cofounded Books & Books, a nonprofit bookstore that brought new literary life to Key West. Blume regularly works in the bookstore, tidying shelves and talking with customers. For many tourists, the bookshop is a destination and a chance

Blume cofounded the independent bookstore Books & Books in Key West, Florida.

Blume's stories still resonate with readers of all ages.

to meet her. The meetings can be emotional. For them, Blume represents their childhood.

Blume's fight against censorship continues. While her books no longer face the challenges they once did, she stands up for books being targeted today. Her concern about censorship can be seen on the shelves of Books & Books. Blume made sure to have signs taped up in the shop to let people know they're proudly against censorship. She still believes in fighting for everyone's books.

Over the years, some of Blume's books have been made into movies or TV shows, including *Forever*, *Tiger Eyes*, *Freckle Juice*, and the Fudge series. But she didn't think she'd ever sell the movie rights to her most beloved book, *Are You There God? It's Me, Margaret.* The book was too close to her heart. She rejected many attempts to adapt it for film over the years. Then, to Blume's delight, the right opportunity came along. When the film hit theaters in 2023, fans were thrilled to see one of their favorite authors in the spotlight again.

Seth Meyers and Judy Blume at the mic at Variety's Power of Women event in 2023

Many of Blume's books still appear on top-seller lists. Her twenty-nine books have been translated into forty languages and have sold more than ninety million copies. A 2023 documentary about her life, *Judy Blume Forever*, won a Peabody Award. Her books have been showered with awards, and she has received honors from the Library of Congress, the National Book Foundation, and many other prestigious literary organizations. In 2025, Netflix released a series based on her novel *Forever*.

Judy Blume may be best known as a trailblazer, an author who always told kids the truth. Her stories have helped generations of readers understand all the worries, fear, joys, and pain of growing up. Most of all, she helped kids feel less alone. When asked about what makes a good ending, Blume said, "I like to leave the reader with hope."

IMPORTANT DATES

1938	Judith Sussman is born on February 12 in Elizabeth, New Jersey.
1959	Sussman marries lawyer John Blume.
1961	Blume graduates from New York University with a degree in early childhood education.
1969	Blume's first book, *The One in the Middle Is the Green Kangaroo*, is published.
1970	Bradbury Press publishes *Are You There God? It's Me, Margaret*, which becomes her most famous book.
1972	*Tales of a Fourth Grade Nothing*, the first book in the best-selling Fudge series, is published.
1975	*Forever*, one of Blume's most controversial books, is published.
	She divorces John Blume.
1976	Blume marries scientist Tom Kitchens and moves to New Mexico.
1978	Blume's first book for adults, *Wifey*, is published.
	She divorces Tom Kitchens.

1983	Blume joins the advisory council of the National Coalition Against Censorship.
1987	Blume marries law professor George Cooper.
2000	The Library of Congress honors Blume as a Living Legend.
2015	Blume's last book, *In the Unlikely Event*, is published.
2023	The movie *Are You There God? It's Me, Margaret* opens in theaters.
2025	The Netflix series based on Blume's novel *Forever* is released.

SOURCE NOTES

7 "Judy Blume Celebrates 'Are You There God? It's Me, Margaret' Premiere," posted March 27, 2023, by iHollywoodTV, YouTube, 1:09, https://www.youtube.com/watch?v=hDrkQVCgM1E.

8 "Judy Blume Celebrates 'Are You There God? It's Me, Margaret' Premiere."

10 Davina Pardo and Leah Wolchok, directors. *Judy Blume Forever* (Amazon Studios, 2023), digital movie.

10 Pardo and Wolchok.

10 Judy Blume, "How I Became an Author," Judy Blume on the Web, accessed August 25, 2025, https://judyblume.com/about-judy-blume/author.

12 Judy Blume, "I Am Very Happy with My Life," interview by Radio New Zealand, June 24, 2023, audio, https://www.rnz.co.nz/national/programmes/saturday/audio/2018895742/judy-blume-i-am-very-happy-with-my-life.

13 Pardo and Wolchok, *Judy Blume Forever.*

16 Judy Blume, "Judy Blume Interview Makers: Women Who Make America," Kunhardt Film Foundation, accessed August 25, 2025, https://www.lifestories.org/interviewees/judy-blume.

19 Pardo and Wolchok, *Judy Blume Forever.*

19 "Are You There God? It's Me Margaret," Judy Blume on the Web, accessed August 12, 2025, https://judyblume.com/judy-blume-books/middle-books/middle-margaret.

20 Pardo and Wolchok, *Judy Blume Forever.*

21 "Are You There God? It's Me Margaret," Judy Blume on the Web.

30 Judy Blume, "Excerpt From: *Places I Never Meant to Be: Original Stories by Censored Writers*," Judy Blume on the Web, accessed August 12, 2025, https://judyblume.com/judy-blume-on-censorship/censorship-places.

33 Pardo and Wolchok, *Judy Blume Forever.*

36 Selome Hailu, "Judy Blume Doesn't Miss Writing. She's Not Afraid of Dying, Either," *Variety*, March 30, 2023, https://variety.com/2023/film/features/judy-blume-documentary-movie-1235566030.

39 Sarah Larson, "Judy Blume's Unfinished Endings," *New Yorker*, April 25, 2023, https://www.newyorker.com/culture/persons-of-interest/judy-blumes-unfinished-endings.

SELECTED BIBLIOGRAPHY

"Banned Books Week." American Library Association, accessed May 25, 2025. https://www.ala.org/bbooks/banned.

Bergstein, Rachelle. *The Genius of Judy: How Judy Blume Rewrote Childhood for All of Us*. One Signal/Atria, 2024.

"Feminism: The Second Wave." National Women's History Museum, June 18, 2020. https://www.womenshistory.org/exhibits/feminism-second-wave.

Gottlieb, Amy, "Judy Blume." The Shalvi/Hyman Encyclopedia of Jewish Women, Jewish Women's Archive, June 23, 2021. https://jwa.org/encyclopedia/article/blume-judy.

Hailu, Selome. "Judy Blume Doesn't Miss Writing. She's Not Afraid of Dying, Either." *Variety*, March 30, 2023. https://variety.com/2023/film/features/judy-blume-documentary-movie-1235566030/.

"Judy Blume Interview: On Her Writing Career & Fighting Against Censorship." Posted April 21, 2023 by Life Stories. YouTube. https://www.youtube.com/watch?v=2xEP6RFXwqQ.

Judy Blume on the Web. Accessed August 25, 2025. judyblume.com.

Larson, Sarah. "Judy Blume's Unfinished Endings." *New Yorker*, April 25, 2023. https://www.newyorker.com/culture/persons-of-interest/judy-blumes-unfinished-endings.

"NCAC's Book Censorship Action Kit." National Coalition Against Censorship, September 25, 2017. https://ncac.org/resource/book-censorship-toolkit.

Richards, Linda. "January Interview: Judy Blume." *Contemporary Literary Criticism*, no. 325 (2012). *Gale Literature Resource Center.* Originally published in *January Magazine*, 1998.

Winer, Laurie. "Interview with Judy Blume." Goodreads.com, June 2, 2015. https://www.goodreads.com/interviews/show/1037.Judy_Blume.

LEARN MORE

Career Girls: Writer
https://www.careergirls.org/careers/writer/

Ellis, Christina, Renee Ellis, Edha Gupta, Ben Hodge, Patricia Jackson, and Olivia Pituch. *Ban This! How One School Fought Two Book Bans and Won (and How You Can Too).* Zest Books, 2025.

Judy Blume on the Web: Kids Page
https://judyblume.com/judy-blume-for-kids/

McGraw, Sally. *Book Bans: Reading Under Siege.* Lerner Publications, 2026.

National Coalition Against Censorship. *A Kids Book About Banned Books.* DK Children, 2025.

Reading Rockets: Judy Blume
https://www.readingrockets.org/people-and-organizations/judy-blume

Shepherd, Crown. *Changemakers in the Arts and Literature: Women Leading the Way.* Lerner Publications, 2024.

INDEX

PHOTO ACKNOWLEDGMENTS

Image credits: AP Photo/Mary Martin, p. 2; AP Photo/Chris Pizzello, p. 6; Unique Nicole/GA/The Hollywood Reporter via Getty Images, p. 8; Amy Cicconi/Alamy, p. 11; Bettmann Archive/Getty Images, pp. 12, 25, 31; David McLane/New York Daily News via Getty Images, p. 14; Universal Art Archive/Alamy, p. 16; Rob Kim/Getty Images, p. 19; Jane Tarbox/The Denver Post via Getty Images, p. 21; Ed Maker/The Denver Post via Getty Images, p. 23 (both); Bill Tompkins/Getty Images, p. 24; Faina Gurevich/Shutterstock, p. 26; Evening Standard/Hulton Archive/Getty Images, p. 27; AP Photo, p. 29; John Nacion/Getty Images, p. 32; Rob O'Neal/The Key West Citizen via AP, p. 34; Johnny Louis/WireImage, p. 35; The Photo Works/Alamy, p. 36; Bernard Weil/Toronto Star via Getty Images, p. 37; Theo Wargo/Getty Images, p. 38.

Cover: Victoria Sirakova/Getty Images.